T0304564

MEN & SLEEP

Jay Besemer

meekling press 2023

Meekling Press
Chicago, IL
meeklingpress.com

Printed in the USA.

Cover art: "The Night of the Divine Tailor" by Jay Besemer.

ISBN 978-1-950987-27-6

Library of Congress Control Number: 2022949903

The two sections of this book are each self-contained long poems, but each page can also be read as a discrete yet interrelated poem. Both long poems are also related to one another.

The Book of Trees was composed using a variant on the erasure method applied to a source text. Words in this poem come from *The Rational Method in Reading (Second Reader)* by Edward G. Ward assisted by Ellen E. Kenyon-Warner, published 1894-1908 by Silver, Burdett & Co., Boston

Men & Sleep was composed using the same method applied to a different source text. This poem uses words from *Germs of Mind in Plants,* by R.H. Francé, published in 1905 by Charles H. Kerr Co., Chicago.

THE BOOK OF TREES

Among the leaves a root.

A great wonder awakens,
great eyes stand open in the wood—

walk through rottenness

                                        all red to sprain & kill.

                          In parks, various large limbs,
                    wounded growths, woody tissues.

Come to the cooler woods
to paint their assemblage
bright & strong
in countless somber tints,
the color of the entire season.

Tiny leaves to the light.

Come, frost
brisk oxygen of countless hues.

4

A tiny tree—the first.

Your astonishing search develops.

> Do you even notice the nation's tree-hold,
> the roots of a knife,
> both *of* the ground & *out of* the ground?

You find a pine tree,
a floating pine.

Between oaks,
poplars learn
the smallest swelling,
the sticky water
for the hope of their duty :

to seek color
to learn how.

Trees in winter have lost their things
to give away the secret.

                                     Quite small, you will go completely inside
                                                  further inside
                                        dark & wholly dead to growth ;

run toward the center
like a bicycle wheel,
tough & adding to that hard,
dark summer.

How can you complain?

There are trees.

                                        From a distance, a broad tree is a king,
                                           the likely twigs & others like that,
                                                      like white crowns,
                                                        big red points,

spearheads buried upon a slope
from the days of greenness.

Within men there are also trees—
they carry seeds
their heaven, carried abroad
their pods far from home—

                                        trees like cats
                                            weeping

such trees...

Teeth are replaced with broad leaves,
warm orange states & lemon trees.

                                          Such trees!

The leaves narrow, to wind & grow.

Cherry trees—
much gum & leaf, the cherry tree.

Boy cherry trees spread smooth & grow on.

All boys are cherry trees,
all cherry trees green with odor.

Friend :
a face of bark on young skin,
a green moist & soft.

                                    Growing cherry trees,
                            the tender, wounded wood.

                            The dead rubbed thin.

Rings reach farthest
out to open the side.

                                        Buds within, swelling,
                                 short shaded buds buried,
                      that the other buds leave alone,

rough & falling
scars, & the end.

A huge tulip-man takes shelter
buttoned to the tree,

winter gloves & his clothes,
harsh coat upon the earth

like summer flowers, blue & even.

You are both male & female
in a mosslike angle where
the red globes join
from the longer twig.

                              Male & female the same individual
                                   distinct as a single tree—

The oak tree
the hole in it.

                                        Hexagon sides & fairies,
                                            their winter need
                                          & their industry set.

wax & wood,

a hole inside them.

Our queer lives in the pear trees,
farmers of our time,
of friends,
the up & down move.

                                        Queer lives never sleeping,
                                          the glare of such fellows
                                              safe in the forest.

Warm in the woods,
feel the little tune.

Her deep-deep woods,
little house in a great huge bowl.

> She tastes there—that there she tastes
>   looks about ;
>   she sits up on that
>   sits up on that
>   & breaks the bottom out.

She lies there, only child :
small with them,
tasting where she is.

She sits up
she stands & looks.

Father's orchard, humming
nothing but humming.

> It should rhyme with my tongue, heavily,
> my busy flowers & our door.

> > The vine is a comfort,
> > the vine & the dovecote.

The bird wins ;
stops my work,
never says a word!

My red plant—

                                        rat says, pig says :
                                          she-ground

                                        rat says, pig says :
                                                she

                                        rat says, pig says :
                                         bread, bread

I will
I am.

Serious animals nibble
eat & suck

penetrate the men
of wood & forests
in such quantities
as to grow years—

                                              with the land,
                              the gray ground beneath

shed the old locks
the sharp winds upon the cedars.

The leaf is done
bare.

                                        Winter's cool, dry places,
                                        entirely closing, lose their oaks.

Certain trees uncover
the autumn
a total loss
in the form of lost seasons.

Silver winter states & trees,
the plum-white snow

great green blossoms—

their sharp eyes come in
& do nothing, sharply

                                                  bells upon oaks
                                                      for real.

The forester calls four saplings.

One & two form a tall spreading tree ;
the places divide closer to the ground.

Hundreds, up in the woods,
instruments on the banks.

A time of falling & yellow :
see & easily examine how clean.

                              Trees still bare
              look into the place of rustling
                           beneath the shed.

A leaf spread out :
a platter of the sky

smooth

a baby's face, shallow & sharp
as a five-pointed star.

MEN & SLEEP

In a portion of the presence
lovers of reeds & alder trees

deafening old swamps & years

impenetrable

primitive

a little book, thawed out into syllables
flowers that nod with the cities at night

the sleep of marvels,
of the uncle of shrewd shade
whose fantasies are tales
images of deep forest

mortals filled with dim philosophy
dig the same dust
in playful wisdom
unveiling the remnant of animate story

chance animals
a man
a mania maintained

the botanist of our corpses
was held to terror,

disappeared into labels
with the shape of fruit
complete & estranged

the secret judgment of life

we frighten,
we look closely :

a hair, a host
a part, a way

snails

great phenomena
unexpected songs &
the wholly different tree

infinite direction
& narrow perspective

we understand it ;
this vision concealed
special forms

life must gather strange relations

we study lovers
& show why

modern beings refuse
friendly attention & patience

sufficient time with twigs, fruit & matter
the thousands rush
& scramble

they are the beginning
the dancing disc of change

the superficial man will rise
& disappear
with quivering muscles

the pressure of sap-filled organs
open throttle

the fact of the root
to accomplish its search
the nearness of sensation

turn everything to ego

attraction of earth
a gigantic task of tendrils
cords of opportunity
impossible to climb

search & test
trembling for prey
favorable support
new life & heart

a little piece of paper,
plain & bare

still sleeping

sentient creatures & night

wilted flowers announce change
& sensitive weather

frost sloping outwards

men & sleep

too heavy a life

if carried shyly, speak of sleep

shake the rain moving that little bush

hot gardens respond
rise to this touch
rough

the body forgotten

our gentle locust, finally all leaf
bend down with ample forcing

the sacred bush
round & poetic
a holy puzzle

the tame land &
the green shadows
in some hot forest

scholars of the mesh, come in
the edges of every star
awaken

six people springing around
like little spoons
in the field of touch

one mystery in the garden

please show us the lover
who gives the same touch,
this somewhat painful bloom
in the need to act

mysterious actions,
secret & graceful

I cannot forsake the fallen
those strange calls

the exhibition of attention
six-legged mother
a thread in a tube

a scheme

heliotropism, upward
the position of philosophy

just demands & exertions
robbing & murdering
the stiff imagination

truly curious
tempting touch
feel
lucky insect

larger insect rolls around
in dragon butter
smelling of meat

dry stomachs
stomachs eating beef
inexhaustible as hair

disgusting rock
pink & sticky
lover vessel

stench of proximity
sun & action
this rooted wind

the muscles of words
slow as our animals

that puzzling odor
of obstacles

every year a flesh & sap certainty
subterranean silky kiss

a little damp stranger
smells of interest & scales
light
tiny holes
the crawling host

transformation

greedily suck
ghost-slit tongues & head

the inner life
dreamed of in the bodies

lift my tranquil stream

injured
torn through by darkness

react to the outer world ;
the outer world
with more activity

recognize
& continually respond to received expressions

limited considerations of required form

to leaves & the suction of time
undermined

not only the described or understood

the first of our apparatus is a little peg
how perfect
we are our complications

our insects, crabs & bladder
a few hairs & life events
a sense of functioning necessarily

all that work

affect them, attract them
stir the glands
excite the spores

most sensitive on the nose
the astonishing scent of the book

this preliminary necessity

great delicacy
natural leadership

concealed life
woods & more

revolution, concern, action
leaves of light
the violet pain—

all come to exist

a little appetite,
poetic & woven from life
a dark bombardment

twist
enjoy the turn

absorb, know

forester too thin
& beseeching
turning into dark earth

once matter was green
& puzzling

now...

one can say a phrase,
which determines light
light & organs
deep light

the best is much-abused
we have an example
we have almost all
the sensitive leaves of light

a strange thought
eager question

organs, sensitive places

display of color has its value

come visiting this superfluous flower
sprinkled with insects

the sexual autumn

perhaps
perhaps the light is only conjecture

that new fruit
clings to the light
to all earth

denying its form to adapt

that smell, hidden
in living knowledge

the glass model of a locomotive
the inner skin thin as sense

the tip of things known,
which a nerve could be

irritable hairs, scattered hairs

the sensitive protoplasmic mechanism

cells
cells
a little rod of flesh

in the outside end of the known
the outside still in the dark

proper

squeeze the underside of value & utility

call the two-lobed organs
they close up like a bear

pliable machine
the little animal needle

two valves

every lover arises
through the external world
their power of touch & freedom

Newton existed as a fir
this tree
or every tree
can teach
complicated calculations

these men are sensitive
to sensitiveness
& existence

men of the lower water
keep their heads erect
find every snail in space
placed upon the body

but how

a sensitive place
resisting the attraction of crabs
an apparatus for a nerve

the middle sense

proper or irregular operation
unable to stand & experiment

know the sand, the old process
play the part close to the earth

satisfaction

results with animals

certain question
responsive to relations of the light

young as the sand in the ear
the substance of irritation

right & wrong
the necessary marvel
& the modern veil

I must seek an apparatus
helpless & correct
my roots robbed by cunning

cold young facts
considered remarkable
according to gravity

the first fact manifest :
unfavorable news
its counterpart school

we the injured,
rattling our wisdom,
are productive & pessimistic

we are incomplete

nature turns, responding
to its denied question

we know this world :
small quantities

we know the favorite salt on the hand

the jest
the dominating purpose
of eyes

certain lively drops
of morning
hiding & darkness together

in the tubes it is quiet
there rises a forest
& intense pleasure

the acid fern
& the egg of water
do not hear

the slightest metaphor
is not attractive

nothing to make sense loud

tones like the fishes' call

our better flower

have thoughts
of intelligible hairs
the external of all we see

metals & recent words
imperfect universe
of always possible energy

this thing, this sleepless cold thought
coming into warned earth
witch-craft of adjustment
the same smell

half-emerald
oversensitive crevices
strawberries

adjustment, adjustment!

yes
old walls blossom for shade

what are we

nothing, except seeds

cautiously we pass through feeling
or time bent artificially

we know there are laws
absent from ourselves

the external form of internal forces
destroyed exterior of a certain order
form without creature

a certain general obstacle
in a definite fixed spiral
our fathers' school-teachers
upon the back

conscious bodies fixed once

we must Other also
we will discover our own Who

the gold road
before it was wrecked

now it appears & we will follow

the forms that we move & bend
do not react

we notice we can touch
with the eye

this is the place

they are together in the human body
yes
yes
they adapt

beginning slowly
cut around this fact closely

describe it surrounding the tiny place

exhausted children in millet
like old apothecaries

father is wounded

suddenly the broken moment begins again
creates interest with these nerves

influences a secret cell
exposed
metal & human bodies

a provisional assistance

the modest world
discovered
the existence of irritation
long ago

through infinite walls, touch hands
through communication
life activities & trans-apparatus

something to designate
by simpler & more capable riddles

we are the Monad
not to be denied

things may be
wholly more complicated

we come there
the human being, all action
sorry & naïve
unhesitatingly mortal
immortal

equally dead

so much stress
conflict & perfume

I must possess every reaction
self-erection
dogma of theories in motion
& my involuntary crushing
& burning

heating of iron by
strange behavior
perspective & sorrow
& every painful session in memory

good animal sign,
consciousness in the other hand

all the signs of convulsive trees

many creatures appear novel
admit much more than this
to the plants

exchange physical forces
in the manner that human life
will call whole

we wish those small
facts & tentacles
the branches & thick
hairy marvelous

impenetrable instinct
acts exceeded by mistletoe
in the dead cold

do not obey
dig life
own life
orchids fitted to act

the theory skillfully pressed
used & living

I have life in creative forces,
which can only matter
in the becoming

still more borders

frequently there is growth
a man with falcon feathers

the rain fills time,
protecting its own
makes us turn & twist

we will have
the miserably tender little robber
that is instinct

the existence of a new word
a mind to arrive

plants are optimistic

if we are impossible,
I must no longer suffice

impossible encyclopedist
utilize the whole dent of nature

& in relation to primitive instinct,
the artificial word
& the answer

so give
bend & cooperate
this is proof of life :

I am not the same

playing with actions of animals we do not know
old naïve nature & birds
& cold night with clover

cling circular to impossible benefits
this strange individual position

shades of the day & natural events
climb quickly

power is its own question
ignorant domination

start back deep into childhood
suck up an iron handle
be torn in two
if we only knew

hang fast
the unessential eliminated
by misleading & dangerous use

only a quarrel, no battle
tiresome down
into the very depths
of the artificial kingdom

man
his own difficult nature
all ridicule & joke
so strongly twists & bends

sub-animal body

it is in the root rule,
the sleep of twilight

they begin their _____
they take their _____ without regard

broken night in anxious explanation
darkness makes us stranger
in us the green human beam
pushed into the world

fear, or the cockroach-
quick psychology
of the matter
of the arms
a fixed body & spite

a moment's movement
body action & a telephone

dispense with worry
exist without a brain
& notice all children
adapted to trouble

we are united in
gigantic beginnings